THE CONSTITUTION AND THE IDEA OF INDIA

Text of the 18th General K.S. Thimayya Memorial Lecture

ADITYA SONDHI

INDIA · SINGAPORE · MALAYSIA

ISBN 979-8-89233-442-6

The Constitution and the Idea of India

Aditya Sondhi, PhD

Senior Advocate

(Abridged text of the speech delivered at the 18th General K.S. Thimayya Memorial Lecture on 5th November, 2022 at Good Shepherd Auditorium, Bengaluru)

Trustees and friends from the General K.S. Thimayya Memorial Trust, distinguished invitees, ladies and gentlemen,

My thanks to the Trustees for inviting me to speak to you on The Constitution and the Idea of India.

Before I address the subject, I must share an anecdote of General Thimayya, courtesy Mr. Vijay Padaki - apparently in the early 1960s, the General was invited to Bangalore Club by some friends to be part of what was called, curiously, the Empire Loyalists Society. When God Save The Queen was played, General Thimayya refused to stand for the anthem. I am pretty certain that cost him his membership to the society, but knowing him he could not care less. Historically, officers were exempt from standing for the national anthem in Britain because their loyalty was beyond question, but this I think was just Timmy being Timmy - with his finger on the pulse and the ability to make a statement nonchalantly.

The Idea of India is a phrase attributed to Sunil Khilnani, from his eponymous book of 1997. I noticed that he begins his book with a chapter called the *ideas* of India suggesting right off the bat that the idea of India is not monochromatic, but plural and multiple. But it is nevertheless an *idea*, which is the essence of understanding the spirit of a nation. He quotes Rabindranath Tagore to say 'A country is not territorial but ideational' - beautiful words from someone who saw nationalism as humanism. The book looks at the things that people had to say about India as a political entity, for instance, John Stratchey (1885) condescendingly commented, 'There never was an India possessing, according to European ideas, any sort of unity, physical, political, social or religious, nor a nation, nor a people of India, of which we hear so much'.

This position has provoked multiple reactions, especially in the 1920s, as to how India was in fact identifiable as a religious, caste-based, and even a cultural monolith – each proposition that has its own inadequacies. Some argue that our village systems and princely states were based on rule of law and hence, had the essence of a constitution. Some look at the Government of India Act, 1935 as a constitution of sorts. But we are really clutching at straws here. The adoption of the Constitution on November 26, 1949, and its coming into force two months later on January 26, 1950, really then was the singular moment where the holistic idea of India was set in stone - as Granville Austin called the Constitution, the 'cornerstone' of our nation. We did not simply gain independence, sworn to democracy, but quickly evolved into being a republic defined, governed, and administered by a living constitution - where Ambedkar's dream of one person one value (and not just one person one vote) was sought to be codified. This process is liberating - in one of my recent podcasts with Siddhesh Gautam (who is better known as 'Bakery Prasad') told me that for him, the adaption of the Constitution represents a moment of magic and of emancipation because it gave recognition to the rights of the oppressed classes, who otherwise, as he says, would simply move from one master to another. That is the power of the Constitution. To borrow from Victor Hugo – this was an idea whose time had come.

The Constitution begins with the words 'India, that is Bharat' and one has to give due weightage to the use of this word. It is one question as to what the idea of Bharat is - that takes us into a different civilisational expedition. But the fact is that there existed an amorphous concept of Bharat – a bit like Charles de Gaulle's 'A certain idea of France', prone to many versions – that the Constitution recognises, defines, and builds upon. It is not to say that the Constitution is the inception of the idea of India but it is most certainly the watershed in crystallising that idea – the Constituent Assembly debates show the vigorous conceptual negotiation that took place in this regard. Those who criticise the Constitution as being some foreign, colonial document, must realise that this is a constitution that borrows from the best in the world. Importantly, it shrugs off the colonial influence, as the U.K. has never had a written constitution.

To me, that is a conscious distancing from the hangover of Empire. We have traditionally followed English common law and could have been tempted to follow the British model of having no written constitution but simply a set of traditions and customs to fall back on. But I believe that a purposeful election of a written constitution that has many streaks of American constitutionalism, as also many which I would think are organic and belong to the Indian milieu, suggests that we, in 1949, chose to be our own people, to posture our independence and to uplift our own.

Kumud Pawde, who was one of the first Dalit teachers in Sanskrit, at her Sanskrit Pandita Award ceremony is quoted in Veena Venugopal's book *Independence Day: A People's History* as saying,

> I am a woman .... a Dalit and married to a Shudra. In all three cases, I should not learn or teach Sanskrit according to the shastras. But the constitution of my India allows me to do this.

That is the idea of India.

The preamble to the Constitution gives us a unique architecture for India – the foundation that is sovereign - socialist - secular - democratic and republic - upon which are built four floors of justice, liberty, equality and fraternity. Each with rooms of their own – justice – social, economic and political; liberty of thought, expression, belief, faith and worship; equality of status and of opportunity and fraternity, that rooms the dignity of the individual and the unity and integrity of the nation. The legislature is in some sense meant to be the designer of the building - who can certainly imagine and reimagine the structure but without doing any damage to its basic features. The executive could be seen as the workforce who implement this design, meant to do that job with honest intent so as to sustain both the intent of the designers as that of the original blueprint as laid down by the Constituent Assembly. The judiciary could be seen as the sentinel or supervisor of these, of this architecture, so as to ensure that none of the players cross those lines and that the integrity and spirit of the construction remains as it is. The legal community, the media, activists and civil society at large, would represent the floodlights and C.C.T.V. that continue to reveal the goings-on in these premises. This architecture is given to us by ourselves, WE, the people of India giving ourselves the gift of a sacred social contract – as developers, co-owners, inhabitants, and protectors. That is the idea of India.

Aakash Singh Rathore in his recent book argues that Babasaheb Ambedkar was not just the architect of the Constitution but indeed the author of the preamble, and the preamble is the soul of the Constitution. I learn of a pending Public Interest Litigation (‘*P.I.L.*’) to strikeout the words secularism and socialism from its text on the ground that they were never contained in the original preamble. Does striking them out mean we are not socialist and secular? While the debate on socialism may be on, secularism is in fact the preamble of not just our Constitution but of our very D.N.A. - the days we spent in school, oblivious of religious differences (or for that matter, class differences and caste differences – at times, *too* oblivious) defined what it is to be Cottonian, Bangalorean, and Indian. The spirit of fraternity, equality, the idea of merit, the idea of respect for religion, the emphasis on being and doing good and doing the right thing, enjoying the liberty to think and express oneself were indeed part of the personality of growing up here in the 1980s.

In his 1850 book titled simply, *The Law*, Frederic Bastiat, the French philosopher concludes,

> And now that the legislators and do-gooders have so futilely inflicted so many systems upon society, may they end where they should have begun: May they reject all systems and try liberty; for liberty is an acknowledgement of faith in God and His works.

But for us, liberty is at the core of our Constitution. We are inherently meant to be liberated as a species, are we not? I can do well to quote Shelly from his *Ode to Liberty,*

Frowning o'er the tempestuous sea

Of kings, and priests, and slaves, in tower-crowned majesty;

That multitudinous anarchy did sweep

And burst around their walls, like idle foam,

Whilst from the human spirit's deepest deep

Strange melody with love and awe struck dumb

Dissonant arms; and Art, which cannot die,

With divine wand traced on our earthly home

Fit imagery to pave Heaven's everlasting dome.

A fitting tribute to the idea of liberty. Equally, Brazilian thinker Paulo Freire – who writes about 'conscientização' or a critical consciousness - describes a fear of freedom, an attachment to the *status quo* and therefore the fear of change. And there are those who enjoy the status quo of the balance of power. There are those 'who do not claim to be the proprietors of history or the liberators of the oppressed - but simply who commit to fight at their side' – to enable the freedoms of others. What Advocates do, in many ways. Freedom is therefore tangible and elusive, all at once. The American civil rights activist, John Lewis, in his memoir, *Across That Bridge* says,

> Freedom is not a state; it is an act. It is not some enchanted garden perched high on a distant plateau where we can finally sit down and rest. Freedom is the continuous action we all must take, and each generation must do its part to create an even more fair, more just society.

The arm-wrestle for liberty is therefore a play in many acts, with many actors. And is often to be struggled and fought for. Guru Gobind Singh in his *Zafarnama* – or Epistle of Victory – written in Farsi to Aurangzeb after the Battle of Chamkaur in 1705 has these stirring lines to offer,

Chun kaar az hamaah heelat-e-dar guzasht
Halal ast burdan bi-shamsher dast

In translation (courtesy Navtej Sarna),

When all has been tried, yet
Justice is not in sight
It is then right to pick up the sword,
It is then right to fight.

While the Guru perhaps meant this in a martial sense, there is a metaphor to the sword in the Constitution - which is Article 32 – the right to move the Supreme Court for enforcement of fundamental rights is *in itself* a fundamental right to constitutional remedies – the sword that citizens pick up to fight the persecution by the State in all its avatars. And what keeps justice in sight and casts a heavy burden upon the Supreme Court as the arbiter of these precious rights. Of course, the Supreme Court has often chosen not to entertain petitions under Article 32, preferring to relegate petitioners to their respective High Courts, to manage the docket explosion perhaps. This merely shifts the *lis* from Delhi to elsewhere, but the essence of the proceedings does not change. The pursuit of liberty through the sword of justice. Justice is, with liberty, at the heart of our Constitution. That is the idea of India.

Our Constitution, in fact, mandates a fundamental duty to abide by the Constitution, to respect its ideals and institutions, national flag and the national anthem. For every right there is a corresponding duty - for the right to liberty and expression, is the duty to uphold and protect the sovereignty and integrity of India. For the right to religion, is the duty to promote harmony and the spirit of common brotherhood, transcending religious, linguistic, regional, or sectarian divides. For the right to freedom of trade and occupation, is the duty to protect and improve the natural environment, and to have compassion for living creatures. For the right to liberty and freedom of thought, is the duty to develop a scientific temper, humanism and the spirit of enquiry and reform. For the right to autonomy and to live a life of one's choosing, comes the duty to strive towards excellence in all spheres of individual and collective activity so that the nation constantly rises to higher levels of endeavour and achievement. For every right, a corresponding duty. That is the idea of India.

This right-duty axis extends even to the State - for all the powers that the State enjoys, the Constitution by the directive principles of state policy enjoins it to strive to promote an order in which justice - social, economic, and political - enjoins all institutions; that the state strives to minimise inequalities in income; that it provides an equal right to livelihood for men and women (and other genders); to distribute the ownership and control of material resources to provide for economic equity, equal pay for equal work; a legal system that promotes justice with legal aid, a living wage and a decent standard of life; encourage cottage industry and culture; interestingly, to have a uniform civil code and (some of you will be aghast) prohibition of liquor; to promote the interests of the weaker sections, especially scheduled castes and tribes; protect the environment its forests and wildlife; protects its heritage and artistic historical monuments; to promote international peace and security; and to separate the judiciary from the executive. Not strictly enforceable, but a strong value system nevertheless that courts have occasionally read into our jurisprudence. A vibrant exposition of what the nation must look like from the eyes of an ideal State and how it must endeavour to build this beautiful, breathing monument. A utopian but aspirational idea of India.

Emperor Akbar had the Ramayan and Mahabharat translated into Persian, and shared them widely. This should remind us of our sense of plurality. We are one because we are different. United, without being the same, a union of states, federal and diverse, complex and various in our ways. A fine indicator of our diversity is Language. The reorganisation of states in 1956 came about on a linguistic basis, eroding the hitherto bifurcation between princely states and governor's provinces, which paid no heed to the linguistic identity of the people. Potti Sriramulu, also known as 'Amarjeevi' or immortal, for his fast unto death that led to the creation of Andhra Pradesh, carved out from hitherto Madras Presidency, showed that language and culture trumps politics. Professor G.N. Devy aptly points out that Hindi is spoken mainly only in Himachal Pradesh, Uttarakhand, Uttar Pradesh, Rajasthan, Bihar, Jharkhand, Madhya Pradesh and Chhattisgarh – that is eight out of our twenty-nine states – and there too often as second language alongside several native languages, some of which are disappearing with the dialects. While Article 343 of the

Constitution recognizes Hindi as the official language, it simultaneously provides for English to be the overriding official language till such time legislation provides otherwise. The imposition of Hindi has been strongly resisted, especially in the Southern states. E.V. Ramaswamy better known as 'Periyar' was one such trenchant opponent of language imposition. Asked in 1930 whether India was a single country, he responded in the negative, saying India was a just collection of various castes, religions and languages. It is the Constitution, twenty years later, that unified us into one.

This Constitution does not speak of a national language, perhaps keeping in mind that India speaks a whopping four-hundred-and-forty-seven languages, of which the 8th Schedule lists twenty-two. One of these is Hindi. This list includes Sindhi – the language of a people without a state, and Urdu – the language of a people of all states. That is the idea of India.

Ms Mrinal Pande, the eminent journalist who has recently published a book on the journey of Hindi journalism in India, comments that though Hindi has expanded in terms of its usage over the past decades, its soul has shrunk. One is reminded of former Prime Minister Vajpayee's speeches in Parliament as being almost poetic. But now language has assumed a political avatar, as has food and culture. The political avatar is in fact not alien to language in the sense that some of the strongest writing that emerged in the wake of Emergency was really in Hindi. The journals Dharamyudh, Saptahik Hindustan, and others stood tall at that time. Arunava Sinha says poignantly that translation is the language of democracy

- if India has to walk together, we must talk to and understand each other and voraciously translate regional languages into each other.

Language, region and culture are paramount indicators of identity. In referring to the Sindhis earlier, I was really referring to the status of migrants in general, and Partition migrants in particular. Ours is a Punjabi family that migrated at Partition from Quetta and Lahore. Having been born in Bangalore, I have more recently began to wonder about my own identity. Our predicament is that of André – the protagonist in Florian Zeller's stirring play *The Height of the Storm.* Confronted with the debilitating crossroads in his life, he asks viscerally,

> There must be some sense to all this! Isn't there? If not, what is my position? What is my position here? What is my position? My position! What is my position here? My position. Here. What is it? My position.... What is it?

I hope you will permit me some self-indulgence. More Kannadiga than Punjabi, entirely South Indian but living mostly in Delhi, thinking in English with Bangalore as the only native place. Now that is an identity crisis of sorts. But this is where I have personally found that I am defined by two things - Cottons[1] and the Constitution. They give me an identity that transcends the 'narrow domestic walls' that Tagore spurns, in

1 Bishop Cotton Boys' School, Bangalore, where I studied from 1984-'93 and whose alumni organise the General Thimayya Memorial Lectures

seeking that heaven of freedom into which our country can awake. An India of plurality, tolerance, and humanism. In that sense, the constitution gives many of us an identity – it is therefore in itself the idea of being Indian.

Ashoka the Great converted to Buddhism in the 3rd century B.C., as did Ambedkar, over two thousand years later, though for very different reasons. Ashoka grew to abjure violence and his life offers a message today. Society at large is growing increasingly violent with reducing respect for the rule of law, with a diminishing tolerance of the rights and space of others. Violence does violence to the spirt of a constitution. The Edict Project of the Ashoka University, in collaboration with the musician activist T.M. Krishna, is seeking to reiterate the principles of the great king. There is one from the 12th rock edict *circa* 250 B.C. that is referred in Allan Sealy's book which has stayed with me,

> Watch your tongue. Glorify your own faith and you do it harm. Praise other faiths, don't slight them. Mix with others, learn from them. This way you honour your own faith and benefit every other.

Beautiful, simple words, reminiscent of Patanjali's Sutra. It is fitting that Sealy's book is called *Asoka: A Sutra*. I wonder what Ashoka would have felt about the snarling lions that are now mounted over Parliament. (I learn that a P.I.L. was recently filed, claiming that they violated the National Emblems Act, and was dismissed by the Supreme Court, observing orally that their aggression is a matter of perception.) Some might say this represents a new India that is assertive and will not be bulldozed – the attitude that Virat Kohli brought to the cricket field as captain, often snapping and cursing in the name of leadership. Others may rue the vanishing pacifist Gandhian stoicism that gave India pride of place for an ideology that was hitherto rare and untested - especially at the time when the world was at war for a second time – the idea of Ahimsa. I would like to think the latter is more the idea of India.

The Constitution is, in many ways, Sufi – I do not say this in any religious sense, but in the sense that it permits for all religion and is itself embedded in being righteous, spiritual, and good (without being aligned with religion itself). For whom conscience trumps religion. Rumi, in *The Masnavi* (in translation by Jawid Mojaddedi), says that while the warriors stand to the King's left and the treasurer and scribes to the right, the Sufis are seated straight in front as they serve as mirrors to the soul. Our Constitution is a mirror to our soul, and we may choose to behold in it all that's good and right. What we perhaps refer to as constitutional morality. that ought to guide the mothership forward.

Justice Edwin Cameron of the South African Supreme Court, who was openly gay and hailed by Nelson Mandela as a 'modern hero of South Africa', has these wise words to offer in his memoirs *Justice: A Personal Account*,

> The Constitution's commitment to diversity is not rooted in sentimentality, it is based in sound political and social calculation it is true that tolerance and

> acceptance foster human well-being. They create good feelings. But diversity is not only about warm feelings. It is rooted in hard-nosed conceptions of essential public interest. We have to tolerate and celebrate our differences as people so that we can thrive economically and culturally and intellectually, both materially and spiritually, diversity is good for us.

That (he says) is the most fundamental lesson of South Africa's commitment to the rule of law and constitutionalism, noting that the Constitution of South Africa pledges to transform it from a country built on racist triumphalism to one where discrimination was prohibited and where dignity of all was fostered. I had occasion to refer to the judgement of the Durban High Court in *Sunali Pillay's case* in the ongoing Hijab matter where the court recognized the right of a Hindu girl to wear a nose-stud to school, based on her cultural beliefs. In some ways, the Hijab matter is becoming symbolic of the ideas of India– as demonstrated by two starkly differing views of the Constitution on the bench.

Justice Chinappa Reddy in *Bijoe Emmanuel* or the Jehovah's Witnesses case concluded the judgement with these lines,

> We only wish to add: our tradition teaches tolerance; our philosophy preaches tolerance; our constitution practices tolerance; let us not dilute it.

Tolerance and secularism are in themselves now reduced in some ways to tokenism. It was, I think, the actor Mohanlal who said, 'Earlier going over to a Muslim friend's house on Eid was friendship, now it is secularism'. We have now made society conscious of these identities that were earlier our glue, and are now our Achilles' heel. When Arshdeep drops a catch, he is Sikh. When Shami goes for runs, he is Muslim. That is not the idea of India.

Permit me a wistful Punjabi verse here,

Bulleh Shah, chal othe chaliye,
Jithe saare hovan anne
Na koyi saadi zaat pachane
Na koyi saanu manne.

Bulleh Shah, let us go to the place where
Everyone is blind to our caste,
and where none is blindly revered.

In some ways it is easier to define what is *not* the idea of India. Just as you know using sandpaper on the ball is not cricket, fake encounters by policemen in the name of justice is not the idea of India. The remission of Bilkis Bano's rape accused and garlanding them as heroes is not the idea of India. Lynching mentally challenged individuals by branding them child-lifters is not the India. Believing in rank superstition, human sacrifice and discrimination, and killing of rationalists is not the idea of India. The beating and killing of a Dalit boy for trying to drink water from a common pot is not the idea of India. Running J.C.B.s through slums in the name of law and order and urban planning is not the idea of India. Incessant farmers suicides - which P. Sainath writes so movingly about – while we boast of being an economic superpower, is not the idea of India. Foisting charges of sedition on an officer who prevents a political leader from entering the A.T.C. of an airport for trying to force a flight after hours is not the idea of India. Having our fellow citizens indulge in manual scavenging (a glorified metaphor for removing excreta from our drains) in the name of employment is not the idea of India. The idea of India is not the idea of a government or the idea of a high-powered elite. What the commonest of our citizens aspires for as a haven of compassion and opportunity where dignity pervades – that is the idea of India.

Justice Benjamin Cardozo, that great jurist of the American Supreme Court had said,

> A constitution states or ought to state not rules for the passing hour, but principles for an expanding future. In so far as it deviates from that standard, and descends into details and particulars, it loses its flexibility, the scope of interpretation contracts, the meaning hardens. While it is true to its function, it maintains its power of adaptation, its suppleness, its play.

That play is the strength of our Constitution, its ability to be interpreted to meet the justice of the time. The rights to privacy, dignity, autonomy, sexuality, bodily integrity, ecology and many others are rights read into the right to life. It surprises me sometimes to see folks read the Constitution as though it were some municipal corporation statute, without its elasticity or imagination. We have come a long way from the dark jurisprudence of *A.D.M. Jabalpur*, where the Supreme Court upheld the absolute suspension of fundamental rights on the shallow ground of Emergency powers. The constitutional Courts need never feel helpless as the letter and spirit of the Constitution gives them the power of 'adaption, its suppleness, its play' to further civil rights and the idea of justice. Driven, I dare say, by the notion of constitutional morality.

Justice Kennedy, in *Boumediene v. Bush* – a case involving a writ of *habeas corpus* of an individual held in military detention by the United States at the Guantanamo Bay detention camps, came down on the government with these words,

> The Nation's basic charter cannot be contracted away like this. The Constitution grants Congress and the President the power to acquire, dispose of, and govern territory, not the power to decide when and where its terms apply. To hold that the political branches may switch the Constitution on or off at will would lead to a regime in which they, not this Court, say 'what the law is'.

Ramachandra Guha, I believe, had once said that the idea of India is bigger than the nation of India, while the idea of Pakistan is smaller than the nation of Pakistan. In the course of my research for my Ph.D. I found that the institutional imbalances in Pakistan have led to the subversion of democracy. Had its Supreme Court played a more active role and had its army played a less active role politically, its history would have been dramatically different. And remember, they got their constitution in 1956, a crucial six years after us, by which time martial law was already there to stay. This is where we ought to acknowledge the serious role that institutions play in a constitutional framework to make us a liberal democracy. Granville Austin had described the Indian Supreme Court as a proxy opposition to the dominant political regime in the 1970s (with the exception of the Emergency jurisprudence) in the absence of a potent political opposition. Here I pay tribute not only to active institutions such as the Supreme Court, the bureaucracy, the media and others that have kept our Constitution ship afloat, but significantly to passive institutions such as the armed forces that have kept away from politics. Reasons, for these are varied and I do not have the time or intention to digress into. But I think less credit is given to the Indian Army for having kept away from political adventurism, which has really paved the way and created democratic space for us to grow. The early years and indeed the early decades of a country are where democracy is vulnerable and I think passive institutions that do *nothing* are critically important to the idea of India. When I say do nothing, I mean soldiers who remain professional soldiers and keep out of politics - officers like General Thimayya who stayed away from politics, though politics never stayed away from them.

As much as we celebrate the idea of constitutionalism, we ought to be conscious that constitutions have their own limitations. Justice Cameron speaks of what he calls the two schools of thought - those who feel a constitution does too much and takes away from the agency of people, and those who feel a constitution does too little to make a change to the social politics of the time. There is truth in both. It is typically governments that believe that the Constitution does too much, especially in a rights-based constitution such as ours. The directive principles that cast a heavy duty upon the government, and are in many ways the conscience of the Constitution, can also often impede undemocratic efforts of the state. The churn is on globally - Chile recently held a plebiscite to jettison the Pinochet Constitution in favour of one that was plural and liberal, but the reform was defeated. The U.S. Supreme Court overruled *Roe v Wade* and reverted to an era where abortion was illegal and opposed to scripture. It is now likely to reverse the policy of race-based admissions in colleges. I happen to also be appearing for the petitioners in the P.I.L. in the Karnataka High Court challenging the anti-conversion law, intriguingly called the Right to Freedom of Religion Bill. The courts are at the forefront of this societal churn.

The Indian Supreme Court has, over decades of jurisprudence, assumed to itself the right to inherently interpret and enforce (and some would say even redraft) the Constitution. This is what in common parlance we refer to as judicial activism. The constructs of the collegium system for appointment of judges and the basic structure doctrine to limit the powers of amendment are both judge-made principles. The Supreme Court has held that Parliament can amend the Constitution but not offend its basic structure – which has over the years been interpreted to include federalism, secularism, democracy, judicial independence, the preamble, fundamental rights and the supremacy of the Constitution. It is indeed unique that the two most central tenets of the Constitution do not find mention in the Constitution itself. Judges who decide whether an amendment is within the basic structure are judges who are appointed by process of the collegium which itself is a creature of judge-made law. No wonder then that governments are often up in arms against this form of constitutional law.

This may not be the place to comment on the collegium system and there are discussions on how it can be reformed or even replaced in time to come. But it remains, I think, a unique illustration of constitutional plumbing to maintain a fine constitutional balance in a country of 1.5 billion people, keeping in mind the gross abuse of power in appointing and promoting judges during and after Emergency. Ironically, even with the collegium system, judges often suffer injustice when it comes to their own career progression, owing to a dominant executive. But it has to be highlighted that the Indian Constitution is what the Supreme Court says it is – and therefore the idea of India in many ways is defined and prone to be defined by the judiciary. No conversation on this concept can be concluded without emphasising the role of the Supreme Court and the High Courts, and as a sequitur, without emphasising the method of appointing judges to the higher judiciary. I will be speaking on the Future of the Basic Structure Doctrine at the invitation of the Kerala Bar Association next week where this dimension will be fleshed out in greater detail. But I will leave you with the pithy words of Justice Robert Jackson, who said of the U.S. Supreme Court in 1953,

> We are not final because we are infallible, we are infallible because we are final.

The Indian Constitution is the lengthiest and the most amended constitutions in the world. I have already spoken of the limitations on amendment introduced by the Supreme Court by way of basic structure doctrine. That said, the need to amend the Constitution is obviously inherent, especially in a complex society such as ours with ever changing socio-economic needs. And while there have been some unwarranted, and even unconstitutional amendments, such as the establishment of National Judicial Appointments Commission, which was struck down by the Supreme Court, several amendments have indeed furthered the idea of India. For example, the precious right to education was introduced by way of the insertion of Article 21A, leading to the R.T.E. Act, which has in some ways been a game changer. Similarly, the introduction of Article 371J, which provides for reservation to people from Hyderabad-Karnataka region, I think, is a unique constitutional construct. It recognises the backwardness of certain districts and geographies in the country and provides for their advancement through affirmative action. Similar provisions are available in respect of the north-east as well. I had the privilege of defending the Orders issued pursuant to Article 371J in my role as the Additional Advocate

General and was able to see how the Constitution can further the interests of large communities of citizens by such innovative legal constructs, that reflect the march of the law. The 42nd amendment providing for grassroots representation through the development of the Panchayat system is really the introduction of a Gandhian form of governance that is decentralised, local, and bottom-up, in contrast to how Nehru and Ambedkar saw it as more centralised in functioning. All of this with the backdrop of a federal structure where the states and the Union are to enjoy their respective autonomy as per the lists in Schedule 7. These paradigms co-exist and highlight the accommodation within the Constitution. The manner in which these cross-currents flow is a tenuous case study, with local governments, state governments and the central government often in a tug of war over jurisdiction and finances, especially with different political power centres. The courts are often then called upon to resolve these disputes, as we have been seeing between the Aam Aadmi Party and the Bhartiya Janata Party in Delhi.

The Ship of Theseus represents a paradox where many elements are introduced so as to replace the original design of a ship, that it begs the question as to which is the real ship - the arrangement of new parts or the remnants of the old removed ones? The Constitution could be seen more as the Mahabharat, which has many interpretations returning to a central theme of duty and morality. That flexibility is more appealing and acceptable. These, and other amendments, disclose the flexibility of the Indian Constitution to be able to better represent the needs and aspirations of its people. That is the idea of India.

I read recently of a new draft constitution by a Swamiji which conceives of a Hindu Rashtra, where Muslims and Christians (he proposes) 'will also enjoy all the rights of a common citizen, barring the right to vote, and 'everything will be conducted on the basis of the 'Varna' system'. Dr. M.P. Raju has responded to this manoeuvre that Indianisation cannot become an agenda of supremacist cultural homogenization of India. That is not the idea of India. Now more than ever before, we need to take pride in our Constitution, to stand by it, to engage with it, and not be apologists for it. That onus is on all of us gathered here today, not just those who work with the Constitution everyday.

Of course, there is need to change, and there is room for improvement. It was Saint Basavanna's *Vachana* that said,

> *Sthavarakkallivuntu, jangamakkallivilla*

> *Things standing shall perish,*
>
> *But the moving shall always stay.*

Just so long as the baby does not get flung with the bathwater.

One of the most interesting cases I have done related to a P.I.L. seeking recognition and regulation of intelligence agencies in India. It may come as a revelation to some of you that the Indian Constitution does not establish intelligence agencies in India, and the all-powerful Intelligence Bureau, Research and

Analysis Wing, and others function, in what can only be called a constitutional vacuum. We fought this case to not just regulate these agencies – as should be the case in any country that follows rule of law and as is the case in many other countries where intelligence agencies operate within the framework of legislation (for instance the M.I.6 or C.I.A.) but also to try and provide legal/constitutional legitimacy to these intelligence agencies. There obviously remain gaps in the Constitution and remind us that change is constant and is often welcome.

In his essay, *Constitutional Crisis and Constitutional Rot,* Jack M. Balkin says,

> Constitutional rot in a democracy need not always lead to constitutional crisis. It might simply lead to a less just and less democratic system of government. This is what happens when a democracy effectively becomes an oligarchy, or when a political system slides into autocracy. Nevertheless, constitutional rot, if unchecked, can lead to a constitutional crisis, just as placing increasing weight on a rotten tree branch can eventually cause it to snap.

Alok Prasanna in his recent piece on emergency powers cites Constituent Assembly member H.V. Kamath to say 'Let us remember their constitution can be subverted not merely by agitators, rebels, and revolutionaries but also by people in office, by people in power.' Dr. Ambedkar had echoed this sentiment too – while discarding 'the grammar of anarchy' in protest, he did say in 1948 '... if things go wrong under the new Constitution the reason will not be that we had a bad constitution. What we will have to say is Man was vile.' The onus is on us therefore to choose well. That is the idea of a liberal democracy. That is the idea of India.

Increasingly now, the friction is going to be between that faction of society that believes the Constitution must fit its idea of India and the faction that believes its idea of India must fit the Constitution. Inevitably, sides will have to be taken. With the emerging axis of a cultural revanchism, a dominant executive and a partial media, the Supreme Court and High Courts are going to find themselves more and more in the eye of a storm. How the Courts tackle these vexed issues of socio-cultural and political ramifications within the letter and spirit of the Constitution is going to be critical to the development (or erosion) of the idea of India. Judges have themselves echoed the sentiment that the courts have not, of late, lived up to this ideal as expected. It is too soon to give up and there is scarcely any other institutional alternative. That said, civil society movements, general awareness of the Constitution, a greater exposure to the Constitution in schools and colleges, regardless of curriculum and, I believe, a greater engagement with the Constitution in our everyday workplaces and social conversations, will go a long way in refining our understanding of the Constitution - so that in this upcoming cultural collision, if you will, there is a collective sense of the constitutional idea of India.

I end with what Kahlil Gibran had once said,

> Pity the nation that raises not its voice
>
> save when it walks in a funeral;
>
> Boasts not, except among its ruins,
>
> And will react not, save when
>
> its neck is laid between the sword and the block.

May we preserve our compassion and harmony. May we stand up for our Constitution and its values. May we imagine an India that General Thimayya will be proud of.

Thank you.

Jai Hind.

The complete video of the speech delivered at the 18th General K.S. Thimayya Memorial Lecture on 5th November, 2022 at Good Shepherd Auditorium, Bengaluru can be accessed on YouTube here: https://www.youtube.com/watch?v=6BOOSDYzyj8.

www.ingramcontent.com/pod-product-compliance
Lightning Source LLC
LaVergne TN
LVHW041306150826
845673LV00008B/2759

* 9 7 9 8 8 9 2 3 3 4 4 2 6 *